JAPANESE-LANGUAGE PROFICIENCY TEST

Full N1-N5 Kanji Vocabulary List

Japanese - English

Nihongo Tutors has been the most trusted tutoring institution in the area for over 3 years. We won't fail you!

搜 N5	画 N5	專 N5	潤 N5
search, look for, locate	brush-stroke, picture	specialty, exclusive, mainly, solely	wet, be watered, profit by, receive benefits
黎 N5	廉 N5	却 N5	囲 N5
dark, black, many	bargain, reason, charge, suspicion	instead, on the contrary, rather	surround, besiege, store, paling, enclosure
訴 N5	坂 N5	燦 N5	晶 N5
accusation, sue, complain of pain, appeal to	slope, incline, hill	brilliant	sparkle, clear, crystal
引 N5	嵩 N5	枯 N5	沼 N5
pull, tug, jerk, admit, install, quote, refer to	be aggravated, grow worse, grow bulky, swell	wither, die, dry up, be seasoned	marsh, lake, bog, swamp, pond
濯 N5	扇 N5	王 N5	律 N5
laundry, wash, pour on, rinse	fan, folding fan	king, rule, magnate	rhythm, law, regulation, gauge, control

葵 N5 hollyhock	**審** N5 hearing, judge, trial	**依** N5 reliant, depend on, consequently, therefore, due to	**処** N5 dispose, manage, deal with, sentence, condemn
自 N5 oneself	**内** N5 inside, within, between, among, house, home	**郎** N5 son, counter for sons	**肩** N5 shoulder
請 N5 solicit, invite, ask	**勅** N5 imperial order	**刑** N5 punish, penalty, sentence, punishment	**長** N5 long, leader
到 N5 arrival, proceed, reach, attain, result in	**悦** N5 ecstasy, joy, rapture	**禄** N5 fief, allowance, pension, grant, happiness	**団** N5 group, association
訳 N5 translate, reason, circumstance, case	**猫** N5 cat	**盲** N5 blind, blind man, ignoramus	**塔** N5 pagoda, tower, steeple

穫	harvest, reap
械	contraption, fetter, machine, instrument
遣	despatch, send, give, donate, do, undertake
契	pledge, promise, vow
糧	provisions, food, bread
曹	cadet, friend
帆	sail
茅	miscanthus reed
震	quake, shake, tremble, quiver, shiver
駄	burdensome, pack horse, horse load, send by horse
若	young, if, perhaps, possibly, low number, immature
在	exist, outskirts, suburbs, located in
寝	lie down, sleep, rest, bed, remain unsold
岐	branch off, fork in road, scene, arena, theater
語	word, speech, language
伝	transmit, go along, walk along, follow, report
奴	guy, slave, manservant, fellow
泰	peaceful, calm, peace, easy, Thailand
何	what
庶	commoner, all, bastard

注 N5 pour, irrigate, shed (tears), flow into	**瓶** N5 flower pot, bottle, vial, jar, jug, vat, urn	**耳** N5 ear	**歩** N5 walk, counter for steps
迫 N5 urge, force, imminent, spur on	**係** N5 person in charge, connection, duty, concern oneself	**示** N5 show, indicate, point out, express, display	**胃** N5 stomach, paunch, crop, craw
林 N5 grove, forest	**区** N5 ward, district	**房** N5 tassel, tuft, fringe, bunch, lock (hair)	**妨** N5 disturb, prevent, hamper, obstruct
苦 N5 suffering, trial, worry, hardship, feel bitter	**券** N5 ticket	**剛** N5 sturdy, strength	**洞** N5 den, cave, excavation
粛 N5 solemn, quietly, softly	**壱** N5 I, one	**境** N5 boundary, border, region	**片** N5 one-sided, leaf, sheet

之

of, this

諸

various, many, several, together

樹

timber trees, wood

焦

char, hurry, impatient, irritate, burn, scorch

版

printing block, printing plate, edition, impression

濫

excessive, overflow, spread out

婦

lady, woman, wife, bride

虎

tiger, drunkard

渋

astringent, hesitate, reluctant, have diarrhea

京

capital

抽

pluck, pull, extract, excel

要

need, main point, essence, pivot, key to

床

bed, floor, padding, tatami

帰

homecoming, arrive at, lead to, result in

妄

delusion, unnecessarily, without authority

尚

esteem, furthermore, still, yet

菊

chrysanthemum

登

ascend, climb up

丹

rust-colored, red, red lead, pills

腐

rot, decay, sour

寺	頭	志	但
N5	N4	N4	N4
Buddhist temple	head, counter for large animals	intention, plan, resolve, aspire, motive, hopes	however, but
蘭	限	豊	珍
N4	N4	N4	N4
orchid, Holland	limit, restrict, to best of ability	bountiful, excellent, rich	rare, curious, strange
洸	透	洪	臨
N4	N4	N4	N4
sparkling water	transparent, permeate, filter, penetrate	deluge, flood, vast	look to, face, meet, confront, attend, call on
利	船	侃	兼
N4	N4	N4	N4
profit, advantage, benefit	ship, boat	strong, just, righteous, peace-loving	concurrently, and
闘	峠	針	花
N4	N4	N4	N4
fight, war	mountain peak, mountain pass, climax	needle, pin, staple, stinger	flower

勝 (N5) victory, win, prevail, excel	塩 (N4) salt	憩 (N4) recess, rest, relax, repose	細 (N4) dainty, get thin, taper, slender, narrow
裟 (N4) Buddhist surplice	角 (N4) angle, corner, square, horn, antlers	泉 (N4) spring, fountain	佳 (N4) excellent, beautiful, good, pleasing, skilled
幽 (N4) seclude, confine to a room	午 (N4) noon, sign of the horse, 11AM-1PM	誇 (N4) boast, be proud, pride, triumphantly	耕 (N4) till, plow, cultivate
況 (N4) condition, situation	刃 (N4) blade, sword, edge	斎 (N4) purification, Buddhist food, room, worship, avoid	杯 (N4) counter for cupfuls, wine glass, glass, toast
銃 (N4) gun, arms	劣 (N4) inferiority, be inferior to, be worse	親 (N4) parent, intimacy, relative, familiarity	休 (N4) rest, day off, retire, sleep

N5	N4	N4	N4
拓	著	邑	常
clear (the land), open, break up (land)	renowned, publish, write, remarkable	village, rural community	usual, ordinary, normal, regular

N4	N4	N4	N4
逐	欲	河	慈
pursue, drive away, chase, accomplish, attain	longing, covetousness, greed, passion, desire	river	mercy

N4	N4	N4	N4
皮	返	綺	燿
pelt, skin, hide, leather	return, answer, fade, repay	figured cloth, beautiful	shine

N4	N4	N4	N4
畔	曇	務	葉
paddy ridge, levee	cloudy weather, cloud up	task, duties	leaf, plane, lobe, needle, blade, spear

N4	N4	N4	N4
猛	起	各	独
fierce, rave, rush, become furious, wildness	rouse, wake up, get up	each, every, either	single, alone, spontaneously, Germany

囚 N5	像 N4	騎 N4	院 N4
captured, criminal, arrest, catch	statue, picture, image, figure, portrait	equestrian, riding on horses	Inst., institution, temple, mansion, school
証 N4	僚 N4	罷 N4	喪 N4
evidence, proof, certificate	colleague, official, companion	quit, stop, leave, withdraw, go	miss, mourning
代 N4	模 N4	辰 N4	思 N4
substitute, change, convert, replace, period	imitation, copy, mock	sign of the dragon, 7-9AM	think
青 N4	切 N4	編 N4	飼 N4
blue, green	cut, cutoff, be sharp	compilation, knit, plait, braid, twist, editing	domesticate, raise, keep, feed
葬 N4	硬 N4	背 N4	締 N4
interment, bury, shelve	stiff, hard	stature, height, back, behind, disobey, defy	tighten, tie, shut, lock, fasten

秘 N5 secret, conceal	**擦** N4 grate, rub, scratch, scrape, chafe, scour	**盗** N4 steal, rob, pilfer	**虞** N4 uneasiness, fear, anxiety, concern
薦 N4 recommend, mat, advise, encourage, offer	**寸** N4 measurement, foot, 10	**凍** N4 frozen, congeal, refrigerate	**曜** N4 weekday
柾 N4 straight grain, spindle tree, (kokuji)	**膚** N4 skin, body, grain, texture, disposition	**煙** N4 smoke	**札** N4 tag, paper money, counter for bonds, placard, bid
枝 N4 bough, branch, twig, limb	**峡** N4 gorge, ravine	**階** N4 storey, stair, counter for storeys of a building	**湿** N4 damp, wet, moist
椋 N4 type of deciduous tree, grey starling	**嗣** N4 heir, succeed	**踏** N4 step, trample, carry through, appraise	**去** N4 gone, past, quit, leave, elapse, eliminate, divorce

由 (N5) wherefore, a reason	**年** (N4) year	**緋** (N4) scarlet, cardinal	**神** (N4) gods, mind, soul
残 (N4) remainder, leftover, balance	**加** (N4) add, addition, increase, join, include, Canada	**乗** (N4) ride, power, multiplication, record	**紳** (N4) sire, good belt, gentleman
禁 (N4) prohibition, ban, forbid	**伽** (N4) nursing, attending, entertainer	**灰** (N4) ashes, puckery juice, cremate	**姻** (N4) matrimony, marry
都 (N4) metropolis, capital	**巧** (N4) adroit, skilled, ingenuity	**女** (N4) woman, female	**瑛** (N4) sparkle of jewelry, crystal
両 (N4) both, old Japanese coin, counter for vehicles, two	**精** (N4) refined, ghost, fairy, energy, vitality, semen	**祐** (N4) help	**晴** (N4) clear up

壮 N3	宝 N4	泊 N4	夫 N4
robust, manhood, prosperity	treasure, wealth, valuables	overnight, put up at, ride at anchor, 3-day stay	husband, man
配 N4	倣 N4	掛 N4	恥 N4
distribute, spouse, exile, rationing	emulate, imitate	hang, suspend, depend, arrive at, tax, pour	shame, dishonor
鮮 N4	霊 N4	靴 N4	億 N4
fresh, vivid, clear, brilliant, Korea	spirits, soul	shoes	hundred million
済 N4	恐 N4	紀 N4	警 N4
finish, come to an end, excusable, need not	fear, dread, awe	chronicle, account, narrative, history, annals	admonish, commandment
始 N4	且 N4	計 N4	筋 N4
commence, begin	moreover, also, furthermore	plot, plan, scheme, measure	muscle, sinew, tendon, fiber, plot, plan, descent

週	稀	駆	郁
week	rare, phenomenal, dilute (acid)	drive, run, gallop, advance, inspire, impel	cultural progress, perfume
稿	武	妙	建
draft, copy, manuscript, straw	warrior, military, chivalry, arms	exquisite, strange, queer, mystery, miracle	build
挟	裁	霧	唱
pinch, between	tailor, judge, decision, cut out (pattern)	atmosphere, fog	chant, recite, call upon, yell
尺	叶	署	発
shaku, Japanese foot, measure, scale, rule	grant, answer	signature, govt office, police station	discharge, departure, publish, emit, start from
母	塗	悼	存
mama, mother	paint, plaster, daub, smear, coating	lament, grieve over	suppose, be aware of, believe, feel

娯 N3 recreation, pleasure	冷 N3 cool, cold (beer, person), chill	揺 N3 swing, shake, sway, rock, tremble, vibrate	営 N3 occupation, camp, perform, build, conduct (business)
瞳 N3 pupil	丸 N3 round, full, month, perfection, -ship, pills	欺 N3 deceit, cheat, delude	圏 N3 sphere, circle, radius, range
呉 N3 give, do something for	六 N3 six	毬 N3 burr, ball	猟 N3 game-hunting, shooting, game, bag
清 N3 pure, purify, cleanse, exorcise, Manchu dynasty	谷 N3 valley	界 N3 world	紘 N3 large
咲 N3 blossom, bloom	教 N3 teach, faith, doctrine	邸 N3 residence, mansion	小 N3 little, small

鶏	婚	墨	掌
chicken	marriage	black ink, India ink, ink stick, Mexico	manipulate, rule, administer, conduct, palm of hand
懐	巽	慧	傑
pocket, feelings, heart, yearn, miss someone	southeast	wise	greatness, excellence
検	掲	騒	慢
examination, investigate	put up (a notice), put up, hoist, display	boisterous, make noise, clamor, disturb, excite	ridicule, laziness
幻	殊	垂	別
phantasm, vision, dream, illusion, apparition	particularly, especially, exceptionally	droop, suspend, hang, slouch	separate, branch off, diverge, fork, another
剖	充	礁	損
divide	allot, fill	reef, sunken rock	damage, loss, disadvantage, hurt, injure

恵 N3 favor, blessing, grace, kindness	壁 N3 wall, lining (stomach), fence	蔵 N3 storehouse, hide, own, have, possess	異 N3 uncommon, queerness, strangeness, wonderful
笑 N3 laugh	秩 N3 regularity, salary, order	進 N3 advance, proceed, progress, promote	枢 N3 hinge, pivot, door
暖 N3 warmth	陛 N3 highness, steps (of throne)	償 N3 reparation, make up for, recompense, redeem	具 N3 tool, utensil, means, possess, ingredients
液 N3 fluid, liquid, juice, sap, secretion	恋 N3 romance, in love, yearn for, miss, darling	総 N3 general, whole, all, full, total	普 N3 universal, wide(ly), generally, Prussia
培 N3 cultivate, foster	萩 N3 bush clover	司 N3 director, official, govt office, rule, administer	領 N3 jurisdiction, dominion, territory, fief, reign

劍 N3 sabre, sword, blade, clock hand	**浸** N3 immersed, soak, dip, steep, moisten, wet, dunk	**挿** N3 insert, put in, graft, wear (sword)	**戒** N3 commandment
核 N3 nucleus, core, kernel	**耐** N3 -proof, enduring	**慮** N3 prudence, thought, concern, consider, deliberate	**町** N3 village, town, block, street
暑 N3 sultry, hot, summer heat	**泣** N3 cry, weep, moan	**拝** N3 worship, adore, pray to	**査** N3 investigate
晋 N3 advance	**縁** N3 affinity, relation, connection, edge, border	**度** N3 degrees, occurrence, time, counter for occurrences	**好** N3 fond, pleasing, like something
酉 N3 west, bird, sign of the bird	**麟** N3 Chinese unicorn, genius, giraffe, bright, shining	**病** N3 ill, sick	**燎** N3 burn, bonfire

炎

inflammation, flame, blaze

号

nickname, number, item, title, pseudonym, name, call

笹

bamboo grass

列

file, row, rank, tier, column

媒

mediator, go-between

直

straightaway, honesty, frankness, fix, repair

艇

rowboat, small boat

織

weave, fabric

危

dangerous, fear, uneasy

鈍

dull, slow, foolish, blunt

考

consider, think over

焼

bake, burning

砂

sand

悩

trouble, worry, in pain, distress, illness

暗

darkness, disappear, shade, informal

衿

neck, collar, lapel

緑

green

抜

slip out, extract, pull out, pilfer, quote, remove

川

stream, river

克

overcome, kindly, skillfully

弐 N3	孔 N3	黄 N3	凸 N3
two, second	cavity, hole, slit, very, great, exceedingly	yellow	convex, beetle brow, uneven
四 N3	鉢 N3	氏 N3	善 N3
four	bowl, rice tub, pot, crown	family name, surname, clan	virtuous, good, goodness
綾 N3	凡 N3	耗 N3	畜 N3
design, figured cloth, twill	mediocre	decrease	livestock, domestic fowl and animals
載 N3	湯 N3	土 N3	虚 N3
ride, board, get on, place, spread, 10**44	hot water, bath, hot spring	soil, earth, ground, Turkey	void, emptiness, unpreparedness, crack, fissure
飾 N3	威 N3	綿 N3	株 N3
decorate, ornament, adorn, embellish	intimidate, dignity, majesty, menace, threaten	cotton	stocks, stump, shares, stock

菌 (N3)	桑 (N3)	象 (N3)	問 (N3)
germ, fungus, bacteria	mulberry	elephant, pattern after, imitate, image, shape	question, ask, problem
琉 (N3)	化 (N3)	場 (N3)	差 (N3)
lapis lazuli	change, take the form of, influence, enchant	location, place	distinction, difference, variation, discrepancy
刷 (N3)	談 (N3)	僧 (N3)	坑 (N3)
printing, print	discuss, talk	Buddhist priest, monk	pit, hole
錘 (N3)	遂 (N3)	選 (N3)	被 (N3)
weight, plumb bob, sinker	consummate, accomplish, attain, commit (suicide)	elect, select, choose, prefer	incur, cover, veil, brood over, shelter, wear
涼 (N3)	忙 (N3)	亦 (N3)	商 (N3)
refreshing, nice and cool	busy, occupied, restless	also, again	make a deal, selling, dealing in, merchant

N3	N3	N3	N3
東	呂	斥	翠
east	spine, backbone	reject, retreat, recede, withdraw, repel, repulse	green
蓉	増	丘	駒
lotus	increase, add, augment, gain, promote	hill, knoll	pony, horse, colt
客	肥	后	怖
guest, visitor, customer, client	fertilizer, get fat, fertile, manure, pamper	empress, queen, after, behind, back, later	dreadful, be frightened, fearful
筒	嘱	州	奎
cylinder, pipe, tube, gun barrel, sleeve	entrust, request, send a message	state, province	star, god of literature
幸	幅	誕	推
happiness, blessing, fortune	hanging scroll, width	nativity, be born, declension, lie, be arbitrary	conjecture, infer, guess, suppose, support

己	湖	痘	校
N3	N3	N3	N3
self, snake, serpent	lake	pox, smallpox	exam, school, printing, proof, correction

卓	慎	個	瑳
N3	N3	N3	N3
eminent, table, desk, high	humility, be careful, discrete, prudent	individual, counter for articles and military units	polish

訓	競	従	憧
N3	N3	N3	N3
instruction, Japanese character reading	emulate, compete with, bid, sell at auction	accompany, obey, submit to, comply, follow	yearn after, long for, aspire to, admire, adore

賃	姿	連	沙
N3	N3	N3	N3
fare, fee, hire, rent, wages, charge	figure, form, shape	take along, lead, join, connect, party, gang, clique	sand

賦	煮	指	伴
N3	N3	N3	N3
levy, ode, prose, poem, tribute, installment	boil, cook	finger, point to, indicate, put into, play (chess)	consort, accompany, bring with, companion

N3	N3	N3	N3
察	叔	猶	朽
guess, presume, surmise, judge, understand	uncle, youth	furthermore, still, yet	decay, rot, remain in seclusion
N3	N3	N3	N3
給	行	早	搭
salary, wage, gift, allow, grant, bestow on	going, journey	early, fast	board, load (a vehicle), ride
N3	N3	N3	N3
謹	医	泌	詳
discreet, reverently, humbly	doctor, medicine	ooze, flow, soak in, penetrate, secrete	detailed, full, minute, accurate, well-informed
N3	N3	N3	N3
恒	晩	陸	炉
constancy, always	nightfall, night	land, six	hearth, furnace, kiln, reactor
N3	N3	N3	N3
紙	零	宜	累
paper	zero, spill, overflow, nothing, cipher	best regards, good	accumulate, involvement, trouble, tie up

詰 N3 packed, close, pressed, reprove, rebuke, blame	**否** N3 negate, no, noes, refuse, decline, deny	**乃** N3 from, possessive particle, whereupon, accordingly	**条** N3 article, clause, item, stripe, streak
簿 N3 register, record book	**稲** N3 rice plant	**迷** N3 astray, be perplexed, in doubt, lost, err, illusion	**胡** N3 barbarian, foreign
淑 N3 graceful, gentle, pure	**敗** N3 failure, defeat, reversal	**酌** N3 bar-tending, serving sake, the host, draw (water)	**漠** N3 vague, obscure, desert, wide
酷 N3 cruel, severe, atrocious, unjust	**弱** N3 weak, frail	**乳** N3 milk, breasts	**伐** N3 fell, strike, attack, punish
陣 N3 camp, battle array, ranks, position	**乙** N3 the latter, duplicate, strange, witty	**陰** N3 shade, yin, negative, sex organs, secret, shadow	**過** N3 overdo, exceed, go beyond, error

<table>
<tr><td>

N3

肺

lungs

</td><td>

N3

析

chop, divide, tear, analyze

</td><td>

N3

回

-times, round, game, revolve

</td><td>

N3

貫

pierce, 8 1, 3lbs, penetrate, brace

</td></tr>
<tr><td>

N3

痛

pain, hurt, damage, bruise

</td><td>

N3

買

buy

</td><td>

N3

腸

intestines, guts, bowels, viscera

</td><td>

N3

酵

fermentation

</td></tr>
<tr><td>

N3

嬉

glad, pleased, rejoice

</td><td>

N3

酒

sake, alcohol

</td><td>

N3

羊

sheep

</td><td>

N3

航

navigate, sail, cruise, fly

</td></tr>
<tr><td>

N3

朱

vermilion, cinnabar, scarlet, red, bloody

</td><td>

N3

銅

copper

</td><td>

N3

型

mould, type, model

</td><td>

N3

玉

jewel, ball

</td></tr>
<tr><td>

N3

敏

cleverness, agile, alert

</td><td>

N3

違

difference, differ

</td><td>

N3

瞬

wink, blink, twinkle

</td><td>

N3

徐

gradually, slowly, deliberately, gently

</td></tr>
</table>

N3	N3	N3	N3
豪	貯	劇	合
overpowering, great, powerful, excelling, Australia	savings, store, lay in, keep, wear mustache	drama, play	fit, suit, join
図	様	浜	絡
map, drawing, plan, unexpected, accidentally	Esq., way, manner, situation, polite suffix	seacoast, beach, seashore	entwine, coil around, get caught in
衆	謝	不	率
masses, great numbers, multitude, populace	apologize, thank, refuse	negative, non-, bad, ugly, clumsy	ratio, rate, proportion, %, coefficient, factor
止	魁	釈	哉
stop, halt	charging ahead of others	explanation	how, what, alas, (question mark)
髪	煩	雨	翁
hair of the head	anxiety, trouble, worry, pain, ill, annoy	rain	venerable old man

双 N3 pair, set, comparison, counter for pairs	**尋** N3 inquire, fathom, look for	**戯** N3 frolic, play, sport	**融** N3 dissolve, melt
言 N3 say	**沿** N3 run alongside, follow along, run along, lie along	**奇** N3 strange, strangeness, curiosity	**貢** N3 tribute, support, finance
勢 N3 forces, energy, military strength	**楽** N3 music, comfort, ease	**納** N3 settlement, obtain, reap, pay, supply, store	**薄** N3 dilute, thin, weak (tea)
世 N3 generation, world, society, public	**寡** N3 widow, minority, few	**噴** N3 erupt, spout, emit, flush out	**梨** N3 pear tree
官 N3 bureaucrat, the government	**則** N3 rule, follow, based on, model after	**甫** N3 for the first time, not until	**丙** N3 third class, 3rd, 3rd calendar sign

N3	N3	N3	N3
療	債	欽	至
heal, cure	bond, loan, debt	respect, revere, long for	climax, arrive, proceed, reach, attain, result in
N3	N3	N3	N3
取	欄	森	予
take, fetch, take up	column, handrail, blank, space	forest, woods	beforehand, previous, myself, I
N3	N3	N3	N3
召	訂	決	宵
seduce, call, send for, wear, put on, ride in	revise, correct, decide	decide, fix, agree upon, appoint	wee hours, evening, early night
N3	N3	N3	N3
万	油	撤	窃
ten thousand	oil, fat	remove, withdraw, disarm, dismantle, reject, exclude	stealth, steal, secret, private, hushed
N3	N3	N3	N3
黛	菫	蝶	昴
blackened eyebrows	the violet	butterfly	the Pleiades

結 N3 tie, bind, contract, join, organize, do up hair	**排** N3 repudiate, exclude, expel, reject	**板** N3 plank, board, plate, stage	**根** N3 root, radical, head (pimple)
猿 N3 monkey	**通** N3 traffic, pass through, avenue, commute	**儒** N3 Confucian	**辺** N3 environs, boundary, border, vicinity
質 N3 substance, quality, matter, temperament	**算** N3 calculate, divining, number, abacus, probability	**延** N3 prolong, stretching	**熙** N3 bright, sunny, prosperous, merry
紛 N3 distract, be mistaken for, go astray, divert	**歳** N3 year-end, age, occasion, opportunity	**擁** N3 hug, embrace, possess, protect, lead	**虹** N3 rainbow
芙 N3 lotus, Mt Fuji	**鈴** N3 small bell, buzzer	**誓** N3 vow, swear, pledge	**良** N3 good, pleasing, skilled

老 (N5)	豆 (N3)	翻 (N3)	楼 (N3)
old man, old age, grow old	beans, pea, midget	flip, turn over, wave, flutter, change (mind)	watchtower, lookout, high building
徴 (N3)	紹 (N3)	多 (N3)	七 (N3)
indications, sign, omen, symptom, collect, seek	introduce, inherit, help	many, frequent, much	seven
飲 (N3)	滋 (N3)	鋼 (N3)	鎖 (N3)
drink, smoke, take	nourishing, more & more, be luxuriant	steel	chain, irons, connection
滴 (N3)	貴 (N3)	抱 (N3)	昼 (N3)
drip, drop	precious, value, prize, esteem, honor	embrace, hug, hold in arms	daytime, noon
檀 (N3)	拘 (N3)	役 (N3)	褒 (N3)
cedar, sandlewood, spindle tree	arrest, seize, concerned, adhere to, despite	duty, war, campaign, drafted labor, office, service	praise, extol

値 price, cost, value	製 made in..., manufacture	腰 loins, hips, waist, low wainscoting	輪 wheel, ring, circle, link, loop
繁 luxuriant, thick, overgrown, frequency, complexity	紅 crimson, deep red	括 fasten, tie up, arrest, constrict	塀 fence, wall, (kokuji)
論 argument, discourse	判 judgement, signature, stamp, seal	泳 swim	第 No., residence
渦 whirlpool, eddy, vortex	昂 rise	駐 stop-over, reside in, resident	設 establishment, provision, prepare
再 again, twice, second time	賞 prize, reward, praise	参 nonplussed, three, going, coming, visiting	莞 reed used to cover tatami

兵	蕉	範	皓
N2	N2	N2	N2
soldier, private, troops, army, warfare, strategy	banana	pattern, example, model	white, clear

字	域	択	城
N2	N2	N2	N2
character, letter, word, section of village	range, region, limits, stage, level	choose, select, elect, prefer	castle

居	雅	荘	気
N2	N2	N2	N2
reside, to be, exist, live with	gracious, elegant, graceful, refined	villa, inn, cottage, feudal manor	spirit, mind

岳	受	旺	腹
N2	N2	N2	N2
point, peak, mountain	accept, undergo, answer (phone), take, get	flourishing, successful, beautiful, vigorous	abdomen, belly, stomach

摘	俳	款	聞
N2	N2	N2	N2
pinch, pick, pluck, trim, clip, summarize	haiku, actor	goodwill, article, section, friendship, collusion	hear, ask, listen

頂 N5	迅 N2	於 N2	舞 N2
place on the head, receive, top of head, top, summit	swift, fast	at, in, on, as for	dance, flit, circle, wheel
九 N2	向 N2	鳥 N2	芽 N2
nine	yonder, facing, beyond, confront, defy	bird, chicken	bud, sprout, spear, germ
栓 N2	廊 N2	茶 N2	俗 N2
plug, bolt, cork, bung, stopper	corridor, hall, tower	tea	vulgar, customs, manners, worldliness
正 N2	殻 N2	手 N2	秀 N2
correct, justice, righteous, 10**40	husk, nut shell	hand	excel, excellence, beauty, surpass
錠 N2	沸 N2	地 N2	践 N2
lock, fetters, shackles	seethe, boil, ferment, uproar, breed	ground, earth	tread, step on, trample, practice, carry through

遼 N3 distant	**左** N2 left	**尭** N2 high, far	**凶** N2 villain, evil, bad luck, disaster
縮 N2 shrink, contract, shrivel, wrinkle, reduce	**歡** N2 delight, joy	**舖** N2 shop, store	**欣** N2 take pleasure in, rejoice
絹 N2 silk	**賓** N2 V.I.P., guest	**干** N2 dry, parch	**少** N2 few, little
序 N2 preface, beginning, order, precedence, occasion	**水** N2 water	**賠** N2 compensation, indemnify	**混** N2 mix, blend, confuse
茂 N2 overgrown, grow thick, be luxuriant	**捕** N2 catch, capture	**難** N2 difficult, impossible, trouble, accident, defect	**成** N2 turn into, become, get, grow, elapse, reach

郊 **N2** outskirts, suburbs, rural area	醸 **N2** brew, cause	二 **N2** two	誼 **N2** friendship, intimacy
診 **N2** checkup, seeing, diagnose, examine	姓 **N2** surname	猪 **N2** boar	訪 **N2** call on, visit, look up, offer sympathy
衝 **N2** collide, brunt, highway, opposition (astronomy)	漢 **N2** Sino-, China	犯 **N2** crime, sin, offense	及 **N2** reach out, exert, exercise, cause
逆 **N2** inverted, reverse, opposite, wicked	粒 **N2** grains, drop, counter for tiny particles	傾 **N2** lean, incline, tilt, trend, wane, sink, ruin, bias	外 **N2** outside
癒 **N2** healing, cure, quench (thirst), wreak	狭 **N2** cramped, narrow, contract, tight	卒 **N2** graduate, soldier, private, die	石 **N2** stone

看 (N3) watch over, see	**渓** (N2) mountain stream, valley	**終** (N2) end, finish	**偵** (N2) spy
整 (N2) organize, arranging, tune, tone, meter, key (music)	**勲** (N2) meritorious deed, merit	**途** (N2) route, way, road	**情** (N2) feelings, emotion, passion, sympathy
穴 (N2) hole, aperture, slit, cave, den	**宴** (N2) banquet, feast, party	**滅** (N2) destroy, ruin, overthrow, perish	**声** (N2) voice
弧 (N2) arc, arch, bow	**窮** (N2) hard up, destitute, suffer, perplexed, cornered	**扉** (N2) front door, title page, front page	**俵** (N2) bag, bale, sack, counter for bags
換 (N3) interchange, period, charge, change?	**睡** (N2) drowsy, sleep, die	**剤** (N2) dose, medicine, drug	**蛇** (N2) snake, serpent, hard drinker

N2	N2	N2	N2
積	棄	揚	甘
volume, product (x*y), acreage, contents, pile up	abandon, throw away, discard, resign, reject	hoist, fry in deep fat	sweet, coax, pamper, be content, sugary
朝	飛	相	抄
morning, dynasty, regime, epoch, period	fly, skip (pages), scatter	inter-, mutual, together, each other	extract, selection, summary, copy, spread thin
渥	毎	冠	跡
kindness	every	crown, best, peerless	tracks, mark, print, impression
庭	順	巻	瀬
courtyard, garden, yard	obey, order, turn, right, docility, occasion	scroll, volume, book, part, roll up	rapids, current, torrent, shallows, shoal
郭	撮	汐	魂
enclosure, quarters, fortification	snapshot, take pictures	eventide, tide, salt water, opportunity	soul, spirit

<table>
<tr>
<td>令
orders, ancient laws, command, decree</td>
<td>協
co-, cooperation</td>
<td>湧
boil, ferment, seethe, uproar, breed</td>
<td>含
include, bear in mind, understand, cherish</td>
</tr>
<tr>
<td>飢
hungry, starve</td>
<td>害
harm, injury</td>
<td>届
deliver, reach, arrive, report, notify, forward</td>
<td>薪
fuel, firewood, kindling</td>
</tr>
<tr>
<td>健
healthy, health, strength, persistence</td>
<td>蒼
blue, pale</td>
<td>友
friend</td>
<td>籍
enroll, domiciliary register, membership</td>
</tr>
<tr>
<td>宰
superintend, manager, rule</td>
<td>亘
span, request</td>
<td>皐
swamp, shore</td>
<td>府
borough, urban prefecture, govt office</td>
</tr>
<tr>
<td>講
lecture, club, association</td>
<td>旅
trip, travel</td>
<td>墜
crash, fall (down)</td>
<td>凹
concave, hollow, sunken</td>
</tr>
</table>

瑶 N3 beautiful as a jewel	**棚** N2 shelf, ledge, rack, mount, mantle, trellis	**研** N2 polish, study of, sharpen	**波** N2 waves, billows, Poland
固 N2 harden, set, clot, curdle	**暉** N2 shine, light	**愛** N2 love, affection, favourite	**笙** N2 a reed instrument
仲 N2 go-between, relationship	**刊** N2 publish, carve, engrave	**忌** N2 mourning, abhor, detestable, death anniversary	**寒** N2 cold
粋 N2 chic, style, purity, essence, pith, cream, elite	**円** N2 circle, yen, round	**張** N2 lengthen, counter for bows & stringed instruments	**捨** N2 discard, throw away, abandon, resign, reject
赳 N2 strong and brave	**誠** N2 sincerity, admonish, warn, prohibit, truth	**岸** N2 beach	**睦** N2 intimate, friendly, harmonious

N2	N2	N2	N2
弔	胸	厚	亜
condolences, mourning, funeral	bosom, breast, chest, heart, feelings	thick, heavy, rich, kind, cordial, brazen, shameless	Asia, rank next, come after, -ous
薫	倖	平	帥
send forth fragrance, fragrant, be scented	happiness, luck	even, flat, peace	commander, leading troops, governor
怪	温	件	疑
suspicious, mystery, apparition	warm	affair, case, matter, item	doubt, distrust, be suspicious, question
礎	悲	禎	匡
cornerstone, foundation stone	jail cell, grieve, sad, deplore, regret	happiness	correct, save, assist
醜	耶	帝	肯
ugly, unclean, shame, bad looking	question mark	sovereign, the emperor, god, creator	agreement, consent, comply with

右 N5	蛍 N2	五 N2	理 N2
right	lightning-bug, firefly	five	logic, arrangement, reason, justice, truth
有 N2	純 N2	失 N2	希 N2
possess, have, exist, happen, occur, approx	genuine, purity, innocence, net (profit)	lose, error, fault, disadvantage, loss	hope, beg, request, pray, beseech, Greece
想 N2	輸 N2	据 N2	学 N2
concept, think, idea, thought	transport, send, be inferior	set, lay a foundation, install, equip, squat down	study, learning, science
准 N2	吉 N2	竣 N2	目 N2
quasi-, semi-, associate	good luck, joy, congratulations	end, finish	eye, class, look, insight, experience, care, favor
嶂 N2	移 N2	斐 N2	員 N2
towering in a row	shift, move, change, drift, catch (cold, fire)	beautiful, patterned	employee, member, number, the one in charge

恩	句	討	墓
grace, kindness, goodness, favor, mercy	phrase, clause, sentence, passage, paragraph	chastise, attack, defeat, destroy, conquer	grave, tomb
硫	関	価	非
sulphur	connection, barrier, gateway, involve, concerning	value, price	un-, mistake, negative, injustice, non-
宏	暢	統	朋
wide, large	stretch	overall, relationship, ruling, governing	companion, friend
玄	嵯	寮	泡
mysterious, occultness	steep, craggy, rugged	dormitory, hostel, villa, tea pavillion	bubbles, foam, suds, froth
寂	魔	較	嫡
loneliness, quietly, mellow, mature	witch, demon, evil spirit	contrast, compare	legitimate wife, direct descent (non-bastard)

拍	蓄	智	夢
clap, beat (music)	amass, keeping a concubine, phonograph	wisdom, intellect, reason	dream, vision, illusion
密	方	仮	盾
secrecy, density (pop), minuteness, carefulness	direction, person, alternative	sham, temporary, interim, assumed (name), informal	shield, escutcheon, pretext
然	呼	壊	狂
sort of thing, so, if so, in that case, well	call, call out to, invite	demolition, break, destroy	lunatic, insane, crazy, confuse
抵	浪	宅	滝
resist, reach, touch	wandering, waves, billows	home, house, residence, our house, my husband	waterfall, rapids, cascade
粗	式	哀	園
coarse, rough, rugged	style, ceremony, rite, function, method, system	pathetic, grief, sorrow, pathos, pity, sympathize	park, garden, yard, farm

N2	N2	N2	N2
松	紋	孟	斤
pine tree	family crest, figures	chief, beginning	axe, 1.32 lb, catty, counter for loaves of bread
答	票	走	棺
solution, answer	ballot, label, ticket, sign	run	coffin, casket
顕	約	脂	桂
appear, existing	promise, approximately, shrink	fat, grease, tallow, lard, rosin, gum, tar	Japanese Judas-tree, cinnamon tree
陪	唆	就	挙
obeisance, follow, accompany, attend on	tempt, seduce, instigate, promote	concerning, settle, take position, depart	raise, plan, project, behavior, actions
他	層	憶	最
other, another, the others	stratum, social class, layer, story, floor	recollection, think, remember	utmost, most, extreme

N5 運 carry, luck, destiny, fate, lot, transport	**N2** 着 arrive, wear, counter for suits of clothing	**N2** 握 grip, hold, mould sushi, bribe	**N2** 打 strike, hit, knock, pound, dozen
N2 省 focus, government ministry, conserve	**N2** 浦 bay, creek, inlet, gulf, beach, seacoast	**N2** 表 surface, table, chart, diagram	**N2** 美 beauty, beautiful
N2 井 well, well crib, town, community	**N2** 料 fee, materials	**N2** 菜 vegetable, side dish, greens	**N2** 巣 nest, rookery, hive, cobweb, den
N2 絞 strangle, constrict, wring	**N2** 溶 melt, dissolve, thaw	**N2** 塊 clod, lump, chink, clot, mass	**N2** 堂 public chamber, hall
N2 弾 bullet, twang, flip, snap	**N2** 和 harmony, Japanese style, peace, soften, Japan	**N2** 作 make, production, prepare, build	**N2** 辛 spicy, bitter, hot, acrid

N2	N2	N2	N2
投	**鯨**	**映**	**工**
throw, discard, abandon, launch into, join	whale	reflect, reflection, projection	craft, construction

N2	N2	N2	N2
德	**惰**	**狩**	**木**
benevolence, virtue, goodness, commanding respect	lazy, laziness	hunt, raid, gather	tree, wood

N2	N2	N2	N2
夏	**防**	**久**	**喚**
summer	ward off, defend, protect, resist	long time, old story	yell, cry, scream

N2	N2	N2	N2
敢	**鎮**	**裏**	**貧**
daring, sad, tragic, pitiful, frail, feeble	tranquilize, ancient peace-preservation centers	back, amidst, in, reverse, inside, palm, sole	poverty, poor

N2	N2	N2	N2
偽	**酔**	**遵**	**泥**
falsehood, lie, deceive, pretend, counterfeit	drunk, feel sick, poisoned, elated, spellbound	abide by, follow, obey, learn	mud, mire, adhere to, be attached to

允	季	変	徒
license, sincerity, permit	seasons	unusual, change, strange	junior, emptiness, vanity, futility, uselessness
顔	惣	欧	訟
face, expression	all	Europe	sue, accuse
覚	農	敦	減
memorize, learn, remember, awake, sober up	agriculture, farmers	industry, kindliness	dwindle, decrease, reduce, decline, curtail
汗	隷	十	臣
sweat, perspire	slave, servant, prisoner, criminal, follower	ten	retainer, subject
揮	棋	巨	盟
brandish, wave, wag, swing, shake	chess piece, Japanese chess, shogi	gigantic, big, large, great	alliance, oath

腕 N2	閑 N2	履 N2	島 N2
arm, ability, talent	leisure	footgear, shoes, boots, put on (the feet	island
実 N2	砕 N2	器 N2	批 N2
reality, truth	smash, break, crush, familiar, popular	utensil, vessel, receptacle, implement, instrument	criticism, strike
抗 N2	風 N2	用 N2	藩 N2
confront, resist, defy, oppose	wind, air, style, manner	utilize, business, service, use, employ	clan, enclosure
弓 N2	如 N2	降 N2	隆 N2
bow, bow (archery, violin)	likeness, like, such as, as if, better, best, equal	descend, precipitate, fall, surrender	hump, high, noble, prosperity
爆 N2	今 N2	孫 N2	惑 N2
bomb, burst open, pop, split	now	grandchild, descendants	beguile, delusion, perplexity

N2	N2	N2	N2
懸	記	杜	章
suspend, hang, 10%, install, depend, consult	scribe, account, narrative	woods, grove	badge, chapter, composition, poem, design
便	滑	天	踊
convenience	slippery, slide, slip, flunk	heavens, sky, imperial	jump, dance, leap, skip
田	碩	還	修
rice field, rice paddy	large, great, eminent	send back, return	discipline, conduct oneself well, study, master
越	眸	服	幾
surpass, cross over, move to, exceed, Vietnam	pupil of the eye	clothing, admit, obey, discharge	how many, how much, how far, how long
見	偏	浅	逝
see, hopes, chances, idea, opinion, look at, visible	partial, side, left-side radical, inclining, biased	shallow, superficial, frivolous, wretched, shameful	departed, die

弘 (N5) vast, broad, wide	**射** (N1) shoot, shine into, onto, archery	**視** (N1) inspection, regard as, see, look at	**尽** (N1) exhaust, use up, run out of, befriend, serve
忍 (N1) endure, bear, put up with, conceal, secrete	**喬** (N1) high, boasting	**朕** (N1) majestic plural, imperial we	**娠** (N1) with child, pregnancy
座 (N1) squat, seat, cushion, gathering, sit	**太** (N1) plump, thick, big around	**録** (N1) record	**権** (N1) authority, power, rights
百 (N1) hundred	**琴** (N1) harp, koto	**廷** (N1) courts, imperial court, government office	**君** (N1) old boy, name-suffix
働 (N1) work, (kokuji)	**海** (N1) sea, ocean	**晟** (N1) clear	**愁** (N1) distress, grieve, lament, be anxious

N1	N1	N1	N1
爵	使	節	矯
baron, peerage, court rank	use	, clause, stanza, honor, joint, knuckle, knob, knot	rectify, straighten, correct, reform, cure
澪	駅	規	麻
water route, shipping channel	station	standard, measure	hemp, flax
辱	遺	餓	宙
embarrass, humiliate, shame	bequeath, leave behind, reserve	starve, hungry, thirst	mid-air, air, space, sky, memorization
名	謙	側	凜
name, noted, distinguished, reputation	self-effacing, humble oneself, condescend	side, lean, oppose, regret	cold, strict, severe
候	奪	改	港
climate, season, weather	rob, take by force, snatch away, dispossess, plunder	reformation, change, modify, mend, renew	harbor

玲 N3	破 N1	賜 N1	反 N1
sound of jewels	rend, rip, tear, break, destroy, defeat, frustrate	grant, gift, boon, results	anti-
雲 N1	隅 N1	牧 N1	持 N1
cloud	corner, nook	breed, care for, shepherd, feed, pasture	hold, have
撲 N1	晃 N1	錦 N1	輝 N1
slap, strike, hit, beat, tell, speak	clear	brocade, fine dress, honors	radiance, shine, sparkle, gleam, twinkle
盤 N1	富 N1	捺 N1	裂 N1
tray, shallow bowl, platter, tub, board	wealth, enrich, abundant	press, print, affix a seal, stamp	split, rend, tear
諭 N1	厄 N1	必 N1	稼 N1
rebuke, admonish, charge, warn, persuade	unlucky, misfortune, bad luck, disaster	invariably, certain, inevitable	earnings, work, earn money

系 (N5)	津 (N1)	定 (N1)	柱 (N1)
lineage, system	haven, port, harbor, ferry	determine, fix, establish, decide	pillar, post, cylinder, support
彦 (N1)	深 (N1)	椎 (N1)	妃 (N1)
lad, boy (ancient)	deep, heighten, intensify, strengthen	oak, mallet	queen, princess
尉 (N1)	吐 (N1)	筆 (N1)	柳 (N1)
military officer, jailer, old man, rank	spit, vomit, belch, confess, tell (lies)	writing brush, writing, painting brush, handwriting	willow
献 (N1)	冊 (N1)	底 (N1)	放 (N1)
offering, counter for drinks, present, offer	tome, counter for books, volume	bottom, sole, depth, bottom price, base, kind, sort	set free, release, fire, shoot, emit, banish
膨 (N1)	集 (N1)	偲 (N1)	景 (N1)
swell, get fat, thick	gather, meet, congregate, swarm, flock	recollect, remember	scenery, view

脳 N5 brain, memory	**雌** N1 feminine, female	**巴** N1 comma-design	**冴** N1 be clear, serene, cold, skilful
包 N1 wrap, pack up, cover, conceal	**横** N1 sideways, side, horizontal, width, woof	**福** N1 blessing, fortune, luck, wealth	**繰** N1 winding, reel, spin, turn (pages), look up, refer to
読 N1 read	**送** N1 escort, send	**点** N1 spot, point, mark, speck, decimal point	**執** N1 tenacious, take hold, grasp, take to heart
護 N1 safeguard, protect	**育** N1 bring up, grow up, raise, rear	**祉** N1 welfare, happiness	**感** N1 emotion, feeling, sensation
倒 N1 overthrow, fall, collapse, drop, break down	**当** N1 hit, right, appropriate, himself	**識** N1 discriminating, know, write	**朴** N1 crude, simple, plain, docile

凌 (N5) endure, keep (rain)out, stave off, tide over	**憲** (N1) constitution, law	**漆** (N1) lacquer, varnish, seven	**救** (N1) salvation, save, help, rescue, reclaim
描 (N1) sketch, compose, write, draw, paint	**政** (N1) politics, government	**昇** (N1) rise up	**昔** (N1) once upon a time, antiquity, old times
付 (N1) adhere, attach, refer to, append	**全** (N1) whole, entire, all, complete, fulfill	**贈** (N1) presents, send, give to, award to, confer on	**卵** (N1) egg, ovum, spawn, roe
丁 (N1) street, ward, town	**迭** (N1) transfer, alternation	**魅** (N1) fascination, charm, bewitch	**憎** (N1) hate, detest
留 (N1) detain, fasten, halt, stop	**義** (N1) righteousness, justice, morality, honor, loyalty	**賊** (N1) burglar, rebel, traitor, robber	**管** (N1) pipe, tube, wind instrument, drunken talk

濃 (N5)	**屋** (N1)	**番** (N1)	**颯** (N1)
concentrated, thick, dark, undiluted	roof, house, shop, dealer, seller	turn, number in a series	suddenly, smoothly
詢 (N1)	**周** (N1)	**輩** (N1)	**報** (N1)
consult with	circumference, circuit, lap	comrade, fellow, people, companions	report, news, reward, retribution
入 (N1)	**高** (N1)	**隊** (N1)	**機** (N1)
enter, insert	tall, high, expensive	regiment, party, company, squad	mechanism, opportunity, occasion, machine, airplane
陥 (N1)	**匠** (N1)	**標** (N1)	**祈** (N1)
collapse, fall into, cave in, fall (castle)	artisan, workman, carpenter	signpost, seal, mark, stamp, imprint	pray, wish
授 (N1)	**拳** (N1)	**垣** (N1)	**祭** (N1)
impart, instruct, grant, confer	fist	hedge, fence, wall	ritual, offer prayers, celebrate, deify

夜 (N5) night, evening	逃 (N1) escape, flee, shirk, evade, set free	案 (N1) plan, suggestion, draft, ponder, fear, proposition	誉 (N1) reputation, praise, honor, glory
募 (N1) recruit, campaign, gather (contributions)	燥 (N1) parch, dry up	飯 (N1) meal, boiled rice	催 (N1) sponsor, hold (a meeting), give (a dinner)
庫 (N1) warehouse, storehouse	薬 (N1) medicine, chemical, enamel, gunpowder, benefit	紫 (N1) purple, violet	缶 (N1) tin can, container
折 (N1) fold, break, fracture, bend, yield, submit	歴 (N1) curriculum, continuation, passage of time	素 (N1) elementary, principle, naked, uncovered	拷 (N1) torture, beat
費 (N1) expense, cost, spend, consume, waste	斜 (N1) diagonal, slanting, oblique	倭 (N1) Yamato, ancient Japan	照 (N1) illuminate, shine, compare, bashful

亭 N5	邦 N1	爽 N1	級 N1
pavilion, restaurant, mansion, arbor, cottage	home country, country, Japan	refreshing, bracing, resonant, sweet, clear	class, rank, grade
博 N1	督 N1	首 N1	党 N1
Dr., command, esteem, win acclaim, Ph.D.,	coach, command, urge, lead, supervise	neck	party, faction, clique
哲 N1	惇 N1	雪 N1	昌 N1
philosophy, clear	sincere, kind, considerate	snow	prosperous, bright, clear
漁 N1	勺 N1	産 N1	疲 N1
fishing, fishery	ladle, one tenth of a go, dip	products, bear, give birth, yield, childbirth	exhausted, tire, weary
砲 N1	杉 N1	戦 N1	信 N1
cannon, gun	cedar, cryptomeria	war, battle, match	faith, truth, fidelity, trust

N3	N1	N1	N1
玖	亥	肪	稜
beautiful black jewel, nine	sign of the hog, 9-11PM	obese, fat	angle, edge, corner, power, majesty

N1	N1	N1	N1
古	幹	購	圭
old	tree trunk	subscription, buy	square jewel, corner, angle, edge

N1	N1	N1	N1
岩	新	濁	優
boulder, rock, cliff	new	voiced, uncleanness, wrong, nigori, impurity	tenderness, excel, surpass, actor, superiority

N1	N1	N1	N1
満	互	企	酪
full, enough, pride, satisfy	mutually, reciprocally, together	undertake, scheme, design, attempt, plan	dairy products, whey, broth, fruit juice

N1	N1	N1	N1
冶	侍	愉	胞
melting, smelting	waiter, samurai, wait upon, serve	pleasure, happy, rejoice	placenta, sac, sheath

租 (N5) tariff, crop tax, borrowing	**硝** (N1) nitrate, saltpeter	**梧** (N1) Chinese parasol tree, phoenix tree	**諮** (N1) consult with
述 (N1) mention, state, speak, relate	**亮** (N1) clear, help	**琳** (N1) jewel, tinkling of jewelry	**脅** (N1) threaten, coerce
足 (N1) leg, foot, be sufficient	**禍** (N1) calamity, misfortune, evil, curse	**潔** (N1) undefiled, pure, clean, righteous, gallant	**幕** (N1) curtain, bunting, act of play
巌 (N1) rock, crag, boulder	**憂** (N1) melancholy, grieve, lament, be anxious, sad	**吹** (N1) blow, breathe, puff, emit, smoke	**項** (N1) paragraph, nape of neck, clause, item
赤 (N1) red	**探** (N1) grope, search, look for	**潮** (N1) tide, salt water, opportunity	**穀** (N1) cereals, grain

N5	N1	N1	N1
牛	比	勁	卸
cow	compare, race, ratio, Philipines	strong	wholesale

N1	N1	N1	N1
臭	旋	蚕	崩
stinking, ill-smelling, suspicious looking	rotation, go around	silkworm	crumble, die, demolish, level

N1	N1	N1	N1
究	夕	火	響
research, study	evening	fire	echo, also N5116, sound, resound, ring, vibrate

N1	N1	N1	N1
珠	導	避	某
pearl, gem, jewel	guidance, leading, conduct, usher	evade, avoid, avert, ward off, shirk, shun	so-and-so, one, a certain, that person

N1	N1	N1	N1
英	掃	堀	嵐
England, English	sweep, brush	ditch, moat, canal	storm, tempest

軒 (N5)	**位** (N1)	**般** (N1)	**鐘** (N1)
flats, counter for houses, eaves	rank, grade, throne, crown, about, some	carrier, carry, all	bell, gong, chimes
兆 (N1)	**邪** (N1)	**痢** (N1)	**穰** (N1)
portent, 10**12, trillion, sign, omen, symptoms	wicked, injustice, wrong	diarrhea	good crops, prosperity
均 (N1)	**掘** (N1)	**栽** (N1)	**所** (N1)
level, average	dig, delve, excavate	plantation, planting	place
循 (N1)	**詠** (N1)	**期** (N1)	**浮** (N1)
sequential, fellow	recitation, poem, song, composing	period, time, date, term	floating, float, rise to surface
没 (N1)	**永** (N1)	**状** (N1)	**彗** (N1)
drown, sink, hide, fall into, disappear, die	eternity, long, lengthy	status quo, conditions, circumstances, form	comet

月 (N5) month, moon	**車** (N1) car	**局** (N1) bureau, board, office, affair, conclusion	**椰** (N1) coconut tree
茜 (N1) madder, red dye, Turkey red	**紺** (N1) dark blue, navy	**呈** (N1) display, offer, present, send, exhibit	**免** (N1) excuse, dismissal
阿 (N1) Africa, flatter, fawn upon, corner, nook, recess	**室** (N1) room, apartment, chamber, greenhouse, cellar	**措** (N1) set aside, give up, suspend, discontinue, lay aside	**李** (N1) plum
男 (N1) male	**伶** (N1) actor	**墳** (N1) tomb, mound	**嶺** (N1) peak, summit
悔 (N1) repent, regret	**橋** (N1) bridge	**窓** (N1) window, pane	**韻** (N1) rhyme, elegance, tone

塾 (N5) cram school, private school	**槽** (N1) vat, tub, tank	**綸** (N1) thread, silk cloth	**貿** (N1) trade, exchange
家 (N1) house, home	**妥** (N1) gentle, peace, depravity	**伺** (N1) pay respects, visit, ask, inquire, question, implore	**佐** (N1) assistant, help
殺 (N1) kill, murder, butcher, slice off, split, diminish	**靖** (N1) peaceful	**該** (N1) above-stated, the said, that specific	**厘** (N1) rin, 1, 10sen, 1, 10bu
銀 (N1) silver	**獄** (N1) prison, jail	**頻** (N1) repeatedly, recur	**対** (N1) vis-a-vis, opposite, even, equal, versus, anti-
採 (N1) pick, take, fetch, take up	**才** (N1) genius, years old, cubic shaku	**孤** (N1) orphan, alone	**暮** (N1) livelihood, make a living, spend time

馬 (N5)	**碁** (N1)	**庁** (N1)	**髄** (N1)
horse	Go	government office	marrow, pith
粉 (N1)	**麦** (N1)	**文** (N1)	**遷** (N1)
flour, powder, dust	barley, wheat	sentence, literature, style, art, decoration	transition, move, change
縦 (N1)	**寛** (N1)	**金** (N1)	**預** (N1)
vertical, length, height, self-indulgent, wayward	tolerant, leniency, generosity, relax, feel at home	gold	deposit, custody, leave with, entrust to
勘 (N1)	**功** (N1)	**柄** (N1)	**材** (N1)
intuition, perception	achievement, merits, success, honor, credit	design, pattern, build, nature, handle, crank	lumber, log, timber, wood, talent
既 (N1)	**題** (N1)	**霧** (N1)	**環** (N1)
previously, already, long ago	topic, subject	fog, mist	ring, circle, link, wheel

益 N5	**竹** N1	**願** N1	**郷** N1
benefit, gain, profit, advantage	bamboo	petition, request, vow, wish, hope	home town, village, native place, district
漂 N1	**構** N1	**求** N1	**得** N1
drift, float (on liquid)	posture, build, pretend	request, want, wish for, require, demand	gain, get, find, earn, acquire, can, may
写 N1	**肖** N1	**倍** N1	**先** N1
copy, be photographed, describe	resemblance	double, twice, times, fold	before, ahead, previous, future, precedence
数 N1	**謀** N1	**埋** N1	**刀** N1
number, strength, fate, law, figures	conspire, cheat, impose on, plan, devise, scheme	bury, be filled up, embedded	sword, saber, knife
評 N1	**蔦** N1	**任** N1	**肇** N1
evaluate, criticism, comment	vine, ivy	responsibility, duty, term, entrust to, appoint	beginning

寧 (N3)	弁 (N1)	脈 (N1)	告 (N1)
rather, preferably	valve, petal, braid, speech, dialect, discrimination	vein, pulse, hope	revelation, tell, inform, announce
下 (N1)	戻 (N1)	亀 (N1)	桃 (N1)
below, down, descend, give, low, inferior	re-, return, revert, resume, restore, go backwards	tortoise, turtle	peach tree
争 (N1)	罪 (N1)	錯 (N1)	虜 (N1)
contend, dispute, argue	guilt, sin, crime, fault, blame, offense	confused, mix, be in disorder	captive, barbarian, low epithet for the enemy
径 (N1)	倫 (N1)	華 (N1)	組 (N1)
diameter, path, method	ethics, companion	splendor, flower, petal, shine, luster, ostentatious	association, braid, plait, construct, assemble
父 (N1)	音 (N1)	蚊 (N1)	野 (N1)
father	sound, noise	mosquito	plains, field, rustic, civilian life

Kanji	Level	Meaning
橘	N5	mandarin orange
責	N1	blame, condemn, censure
茎	N1	stalk, stem
脩	N1	dried meat
岬	N1	headland, cape, spit, promontory
業	N1	business, vocation, arts, performance
市	N1	market, city, town
荒	N1	laid waste, rough, rude, wild
舌	N1	tongue, reed, clapper
吸	N1	suck, imbibe, inhale, sip
汽	N1	vapor, steam
忠	N1	loyalty, fidelity, faithfulness
雇	N1	employ, hire
沈	N1	sink, be submerged, subside, be depressed, aloes
駿	N1	a good horse, speed, a fast person
匹	N1	equal, head, counter for small animals
出	N1	exit, leave
芹	N1	parsley
公	N1	public, prince, official, governmental
脱	N1	undress, removing, escape from, get rid of

鼻	姫	烈	舎
nose, snout	princess	ardent, violent, vehement, furious, severe, extreme	cottage, inn, hut, house, mansion
慣	助	誘	黒
accustomed, get used to, become experienced	help, rescue, assist	entice, lead, tempt, invite, ask, call for	black
宗	藍	銑	瑞
religion, sect, denomination, main point, origin	indigo	pig iron	congratulations
捷	漏	喫	緯
victory, fast	leak, escape, time	consume, eat, drink, smoke, receive (a blow)	horizontal, woof, left & right, latitude
渇	渚	誌	退
thirst, dry up, parch	strand, beach, shore	document, records	retreat, withdraw, retire, resign, repel, expel

N5 尊	N1 供	N1 楠	N1 芝
revered, valuable, precious, noble, exalted	submit, offer, present, serve (meal), accompany	camphor tree	turf, lawn
N1 患	N1 叙	N1 娘	N1 書
afflicted, disease, suffer from, be ill	confer, relate, narrate, describe	daughter, girl	write
N1 旨	N1 迪	N1 奮	N1 舶
delicious, relish, show a liking for, purport, will	edify, way, path	stirred up, be invigorated, flourish	liner, ship
N1 諒	N1 彫	N1 鵬	N1 慰
fact, reality, understand, appreciate	carve, engrave, chisel	phoenix	consolation, amusement, seduce, cheer, console
N1 儀	N1 特	N1 未	N1 酬
ceremony, rule, affair, case, a matter	special	un-, not yet, hitherto, still, even now	repay, reward, retribution

託 N5	速 N1	昨 N1	国 N1
consign, requesting, entrusting with, pretend, hint	quick, fast	yesterday, previous	country
鉱 N1	励 N1	央 N1	刈 N1
mineral, ore	encourage, be diligent, inspire	center, middle	reap, cut, clip, trim, prune
断 N1	侑 N1	摂 N1	民 N1
severance, decline, refuse, apologize	urge to eat	vicarious, surrogate, act in addition to	people, nation, subjects
厳 N1	漱 N1	春 N1	銘 N1
stern, strictness, severity, rigidity	gargle, rinse mouth	springtime, spring (season)	inscription, signature (of artisan)
距 N1	胤 N1	鬼 N1	死 N1
long-distance	descendent, issue, offspring	ghost, devil	death, die

N3	N1	N1	N1
唯 solely, only, merely, simply	**治** reign, be at peace, calm down, subdue, quell	**援** abet, help, save	**箱** box, chest, case, bin, railway car
N1	N1	N1	N1
共 together, both, neither, all, and, alike, with	**宇** eaves, roof, house, heaven	**誤** mistake, err, do wrong, mislead	**三** three
N1	N1	N1	N1
愚 foolish, folly, absurdity, stupid	**添** annexed, accompany, marry, suit, meet	**冒** risk, face, defy, dare, damage, assume (a name)	**押** push, stop, check, subdue, attach
N1	N1	N1	N1
恭 respect, reverent	**障** hinder, hurt, harm	**緊** tense, solid, hard, reliable, tight	**熱** heat, temperature, fever, mania, passion
N1	N1	N1	N1
奈 Nara, what?	**割** proportion, comparatively, divide, cut, separate	**衷** inmost, heart, mind, inside	**旗** national flag, banner, standard

堤 N5	士 N1	品 N1	余 N1
dike, bank, embankment	gentleman, samurai	goods, refinement, dignity, article	too much, myself, surplus, other, remainder
往 N1	因 N1	量 N1	皆 N1
journey, chase away, let go, going, travel	cause, factor, be associated with, depend on	quantity, measure, weight, amount, consider	all, everything
謁 N1	伍 N1	湾 N1	殖 N1
audience, audience (with king)	5, 5-man squad, file, line	gulf, bay, inlet	augment, increase, multiply, raise
麗 N1	附 N1	伏 N1	鹿 N1
lovely, companion	affixed, attach, refer to, append	prostrated, bend down, bow, cover, lay (pipes)	deer
瞭 N1	絢 N1	交 N1	弦 N1
clear	kimono design	mingle, mixing, association, coming & going	bowstring, chord, hypotenuse

享 (N5) receive, undergo, answer (phone), take, get, catch	**亨** (N1) undergo, answer (phone), take, get, catch	**肝** (N1) liver, pluck, nerve, chutzpah	**詞** (N1) part of speech, words, poetry
策 (N1) scheme, plan, policy, step, means	**須** (N1) ought, by all means, necessarily	**菓** (N1) candy, cakes, fruit	**西** (N1) west, Spain
完 (N1) perfect, completion, end	**氷** (N1) icicle, ice, hail, freeze, congeal	**承** (N1) acquiesce, hear, listen to, be informed, receive	**日** (N1) day, sun, Japan
彪 (N1) spotted, mottled, patterned, small tiger	**顧** (N1) look back, review, examine oneself, turn around	**鍛** (N1) forge, discipline, train	**搬** (N1) conveyor, carry, transport
敵 (N1) enemy, foe, opponent	**覇** (N1) hegemony, supremacy, leadership, champion	**主** (N1) lord, chief, master, main thing, principal	**毒** (N1) poison, virus, venom, germ, harm, injury, spite

擬 (N5) mimic, aim (a gun) at, nominate, imitate	**滞** (N1) stagnate, be delayed, overdue, arrears	**帳** (N1) notebook, account book, album	**瑚** (N1) ancestral offering receptacle
立 (N1) stand up	**閥** (N1) clique, lineage, pedigree, faction, clan	**棒** (N1) rod, stick, cane, pole, club, line	**箇** (N1) counters for things
貨 (N1) freight, goods, property	**熟** (N1) mellow, ripen, mature, acquire skill	**稔** (N1) harvest, ripen	**斗** (N1) Big Dipper, 10 sho (vol), sake dipper
散 (N1) scatter, disperse, spend, squander	**怜** (N1) wise	**羅** (N1) gauze, thin silk, Rome	**宿** (N1) inn, lodging, relay station, dwell, lodge
込 (N1) crowded, mixture, in bulk, included	**朔** (N1) conjunction (astronomy), first day of month	**枠** (N1) frame, framework, spindle, spool	**課** (N1) chapter, lesson, section, department, division

面 (N5)	鯛 (N1)	昆 (N1)	塑 (N1)
mask, face, features, surface	sea bream, red snapper	descendants, elder brother, insect	model, molding
賄 (N1)	婆 (N1)	準 (N1)	童 (N1)
bribe, board, supply, finance	old woman, grandma, wet nurse	semi-, correspond to, proportionate to, conform	juvenile, child
瑠 (N1)	壌 (N1)	制 (N1)	甲 (N1)
lapis lazuli	lot, earth, soil	system, law, rule	armor, high (voice), A grade, first class, former
時 (N1)	暴 (N1)	僕 (N1)	鶴 (N1)
time, hour	outburst, rave, fret, force, violence, cruelty	me, I (male)	crane, stork
毛 (N1)	胎 (N1)	鷹 (N1)	麿 (N1)
fur, hair, feather, down	womb, uterus	hawk	I, you, (kokuji)

栗 **N5** chestnut	拠 **N1** foothold, based on, follow, therefore	児 **N1** newborn babe, child, young of animals	興 **N1** entertain, revive, retrieve, interest, pleasure
遅 **N1** slow, late, back, later	畳 **N1** tatami mat, counter for tatami mats, fold	種 **N1** species, kind, class, variety, seed	丞 **N1** help
初 **N1** first time, beginning	壇 **N1** podium, stage, rostrum, terrace	彩 **N1** coloring, paint, makeup	鋳 **N1** casting, mint
榛 **N1** hazelnut, filbert	稚 **N1** immature, young	帯 **N1** sash, belt, obi, zone, region	望 **N1** ambition, full moon, hope, desire, aspire to, expect
軸 **N1** axis, pivot, stem, stalk, counter for book scrolls	重 **N1** heavy, heap up, pile up, nest of boxes, -fold	広 **N1** wide, broad, spacious	吟 **N1** versify, singing, recital

接 (N5) touch, contact, adjoin, piece together	**眺** (N1) stare, watch, look at, see, scrutinize	**曆** (N1) calendar, almanac	**笛** (N1) flute, clarinet, pipe, whistle, bagpipe, piccolo
舟 (N1) boat, ship	**致** (N1) doth, do, send, forward, cause, exert, incur, engage	**額** (N1) forehead, tablet, plaque, framed picture, sum	**技** (N1) skill, art, craft, ability, feat, performance
雄 (N1) masculine, male, hero, leader, superiority	**副** (N1) vice-, duplicate, copy	**肌** (N1) texture, skin, body, grain	**忘** (N1) forget
遭 (N1) encounter, meet, party, association, interview	**色** (N1) color	**道** (N1) road-way, street, district, journey, course	**飽** (N1) sated, tired of, bored, satiate
慨 (N1) rue, be sad, sigh, lament	**替** (N1) exchange, spare, substitute, per-	**軌** (N1) rut, wheel, track, model, way of doing	**輔** (N1) help

班 N3	路 N1	秋 N1	獣 N1
squad, corps, unit, group	path, route, road, distance	autumn	animal, beast
空 N1	鑑 N1	維 N1	架 N1
empty, sky, void, vacant, vacuum	specimen, take warning from, learn from	fiber, tie, rope	erect, frame, mount, support, shelf, construct
前 N1	祝 N1	陽 N1	浄 N1
in front, before	celebrate, congratulate	sunshine, yang principle, positive, male, heaven	clean, purify, cleanse, exorcise, Manchu Dynasty
楓 N1	尾 N1	叫 N1	恨 N1
maple	tail, end, counter for fish, lower slope of mountain	shout, exclaim, yell	regret, bear a grudge, resentment, malice, hatred
創 N1	易 N1	街 N1	弊 N1
genesis, wound, injury, hurt, start, originate	easy, ready to, simple, fortune-telling, divination	boulevard, street, town	abuse, evil, vice, breakage

胴 (N5) trunk, torso, hull (ship), hub of wheel	**遮** (N1) intercept, interrupt, obstruct	**与** (N1) bestow, participate in, give, award, impart, provide	**招** (N1) beckon, invite, summon, engage
惟 (N1) consider, reflect, think	**啓** (N1) disclose, open, say	**眉** (N1) eyebrow	**帽** (N1) cap, headgear
村 (N1) town, village	**秦** (N1) Manchu dynasty	**爾** (N1) you, thou, second person	**例** (N1) example, custom, usage, precedent
意 (N1) idea, mind, heart, taste, thought, desire	**茄** (N1) eggplant	**堕** (N1) degenerate, descend to, lapse into	**机** (N1) desk, table
軟 (N1) soft	**復** (N1) restore, return to, revert, resume	**汚** (N1) dirty, pollute, disgrace, rape, defile	**将** (N1) leader, commander, general, admiral, or

派 (N5) faction, group, party, clique, sect, school	**台** (N1) pedestal, a stand, counter for machines and vehicles	**隔** (N1) isolate, alternate, distance, separate, gulf	**動** (N1) move, motion, change, confusion, shift, shake
暇 (N1) spare time, rest, leisure, time, leave of absence	**磯** (N1) seashore, beach	**倹** (N1) frugal, economy, thrifty	**酢** (N1) vinegar, sour, acid, tart
銭 (N1) coin, .01 yen, money	**扱** (N1) handle, entertain, thresh, strip	**確** (N1) assurance, firm, tight, hard, solid, confirm	**是** (N1) just so, this, right, justice
糖 (N1) sugar	**聡** (N1) wise, fast learner	**悠** (N1) permanence, distant, long time, leisure	**緒** (N1) thong, beginning, inception, end, cord, strap
我 (N1) ego, I, selfish, our, oneself	**暁** (N1) daybreak, dawn, in the event	**程** (N1) extent, degree, law, formula, distance, limits	**媛** (N1) beautiful woman, princess

N5	**N1**	**N1**	**N1**
屯	貝	測	澄
barracks, police station, camp	shellfish	fathom, plan, scheme, measure	lucidity, be clear, clear, clarify, settle, strain
N1	**N1**	**N1**	**N1**
杏	控	者	涯
apricot	withdraw, draw in, hold back, refrain from	someone, person	horizon, shore
N1	**N1**	**N1**	**N1**
際	隣	肉	説
occasion, side, edge, verge, dangerous, adventurous	neighboring	meat	rumor, opinion, theory
N1	**N1**	**N1**	**N1**
窒	鞠	間	染
plug up, obstruct	ball	interval, space	dye, color, paint, stain, print
N1	**N1**	**N1**	**N1**
尿	千	豚	裕
urine	thousand	pork, pig	abundant, rich, fertile

N5	N1	N1	N1
続	一	略	命
continue, series, sequel	one	abbreviation, omission, outline, shorten, capture	fate, command, decree, destiny, life, appoint
N1	**N1**	**N1**	**N1**
侵	犠	琢	漫
encroach, invade, raid, trespass, violate	sacrifice	polish	cartoon, involuntarily, in spite of oneself
N1	**N1**	**N1**	**N1**
球	恕	勉	卑
ball, sphere	excuse, tolerate, forgive	exertion	lowly, base, vile, vulgar
N1	**N1**	**N1**	**N1**
燃	祥	宥	懇
burn, blaze, glow	auspicious, happiness, good omen	soothe, calm, pacify	sociable, kind, courteous, hospitable, cordial
N1	**N1**	**N1**	**N1**
逮	桜	極	紡
apprehend, chase	cherry	poles, settlement, conclusion, end	spinning

茉 N3	抹 N1	人 N1	諄 N1
jasmine	rub, paint, erase	person	tedious
印 N1	法 N1	桟 N1	験 N1
stamp, seal, mark, imprint, symbol, emblem	method, law, rule, principle, model, system	scaffold, cleat, frame, jetty, bolt (door)	verification, effect, testing
斉 N1	庸 N1	采 N1	曲 N1
adjusted, alike, equal, similar variety of	commonplace, ordinary, employment	dice, form, appearance, take, coloring	bend, music, melody, composition
鏡 N1	演 N1	電 N1	痴 N1
mirror, speculum, barrel-head	performance, act, play, render, stage	electricity	stupid, foolish
菖 N1	晏 N1	穂 N1	概 N1
iris	late, quiet, sets (sun)	ear, ear (grain), head, crest (wave)	outline, condition, approximation, generally

傘 (N5)	齢 (N1)	綜 (N1)	征 (N1)
umbrella	age	rule	subjugate, attack the rebellious, collect taxes
山 (N1)	郵 (N1)	廃 (N1)	売 (N1)
mountain	mail, stagecoach stop	abolish, obsolete, cessation, discarding, abandon	sell
罰 (N1)	伊 (N1)	縫 (N1)	拡 (N1)
penalty, punishment	Italy, that one	sew, stitch, embroider	broaden, extend, expand, enlarge
傷 (N1)	芳 (N1)	皿 (N1)	凪 (N1)
wound, hurt, injure, impair, pain, injury, cut	perfume, balmy, flavorable, fragrant	dish, a helping, plate	lull, calm, (kokuji)
能 (N1)	縄 (N1)	子 (N1)	停 (N1)
ability, talent, skill, capacity	straw rope, cord	child, sign of the rat, 11PM-1AM	halt, stopping

覆
capsize, cover, shade, mantle, be ruined

嚇
menacing, dignity, majesty, threaten

脹
dilate, distend, bulge, fill out, swell

炊
cook, boil

只
only, free, in addition

賛
approve, praise, title or inscription on picture

彰
patent, clear

芸
technique, art, craft, performance, acting

影
shadow, silhouette, phantom

併
join, get together, unite, collective

源
source, origin

羽
feathers, counter for birds, rabbits

灯
lamp, a light, light, counter for lights

遊
play

宮
Shinto shrine, constellations, palace, princess

低
lower, short, humble

貞
upright, chastity, constancy, righteousness

展
unfold, expand

敬
awe, respect, honor, revere

塚
hillock, mound

遞	霞	怒	栞
N5	N1	N1	N1
relay, in turn, sending	be hazy, grow dim, blurred	angry, be offended	bookmark, guidebook

冗	委	懲	淳
N1	N1	N1	N1
superfluous, uselessness	committee, entrust to, leave to, devote, discard	penal, chastise, punish, discipline	pure

拙	認	江	携
N1	N1	N1	N1
bungling, clumsy, unskillful	acknowledge, witness, discern, recognize	creek, inlet, bay	portable, carry (in hand), armed with, bring along

兄	匿	県	口
N1	N1	N1	N1
elder brother, big brother	hide, shelter, shield	prefecture	mouth

旭	遍	担	力
N1	N1	N1	N1
rising sun, morning sun	everywhere, times, widely, generally	shouldering, carry, raise, bear	power, strong, strain, bear up, exert

疫 N5	抑 N1	奏 N1	暫 N1
epidemic	repress, well, now, in the first place, push	play music, speak to a ruler, complete	temporarily, a while, moment, long time
甚 N1	冬 N1	即 N1	仕 N1
tremendously, very, great, exceedingly	winter	instant, namely, as is, conform, agree, adapt	attend, doing, official, serve
単 N1	惜 N1	縛 N1	事 N1
simple, one, single, merely	pity, be sparing of, frugal, stingy, regret	truss, arrest, bind, tie, restrain	matter, thing, fact, business, reason, possibly
故 N1	峻 N1	唄 N1	適 N1
happenstance, especially	high, steep	songs with samisen	suitable, occasional, rare, qualified, capable
格 N1	歯 N1	露 N1	慶 N1
status, rank, capacity, character	tooth, cog	dew, tears, expose, Russia	jubilation, congratulate, rejoice, be happy

褐 N5	本 N1	洲 N1	基 N1
brown, woollen kimono	book, present, main, true, real	continent, sandbar, island, country	fundamentals, radical (chem), counter for machines
体 N1	明 N1	元 N1	驚 N1
body, substance, object, reality, counter for images	bright, light	beginning, former time, origin	wonder, be surprised, frightened, amazed
詐 N1	提 N1	隻 N1	芋 N1
lie, falsehood, deceive, pretend	propose, take along, carry in hand	vessels, counter for ships, fish, birds, arrows	potato
態 N1	白 N1	汰 N1	昭 N1
attitude, condition, figure, appearance	white	luxury, select	shining, bright
話 N1	彬 N1	扶 N1	宣 N1
tale, talk	refined, gentle	aid, help, assist	proclaim, say, announce

<table>
<tr><td>

赦

N5

pardon, forgiveness

</td><td>

除

N1

exclude, division (x, 3), remove, abolish, cancel

</td><td>

錬

N1

tempering, refine, drill, train, polish

</td><td>

以

N1

by means of, because, in view of, compared with

</td></tr>
<tr><td>

称

N1

appellation, praise, admire, name, title, fame

</td><td>

潟

N1

lagoon

</td><td>

繭

N1

cocoon

</td><td>

翼

N1

wing, plane, flank

</td></tr>
<tr><td>

巡

N1

patrol, go around, circumference

</td><td>

現

N1

present, existing, actual

</td><td>

績

N1

exploits, unreeling cocoons

</td><td>

趣

N1

gist, proceed to, tend, become

</td></tr>
<tr><td>

迎

N1

welcome, meet, greet

</td><td>

議

N1

deliberation, consultation, debate, consideration

</td><td>

朗

N1

melodious, clear, bright, serene, cheerful

</td><td>

俊

N1

sagacious, genius, excellence

</td></tr>
<tr><td>

蒔

N1

sow (seeds)

</td><td>

形

N1

shape, form, style

</td><td>

次

N1

next, order, sequence

</td><td>

閲

N1

review, inspection, revision

</td></tr>
</table>

N5 活 lively, resuscitation, being helped, living	**N1** 苗 seedling, sapling, shoot	**N1** 溝 gutter, ditch, sewer, drain, 10**32	**N1** 鯉 carp
N1 膜 membrane	**N1** 似 becoming, resemble, counterfeit, imitate, suitable	**N1** 真 true, reality, Buddhist sect	**N1** 観 outlook, look, appearance, condition, view
N1 也 to be (classical)	**N1** 艶 glossy, luster, glaze, polish, charm, colorful	**N1** 衛 defense, protection	**N1** 塁 bases, fort, rampart, walls, base(ball)
N1 備 equip, provision, preparation	**N1** 解 unravel, notes, key, explanation	**N1** 賢 intelligent, wise, wisdom, cleverness	**N1** 佑 help, assist
N1 胆 gall bladder, courage, pluck, nerve	**N1** 疎 alienate, rough, neglect, shun, sparse	**N1** 努 toil, diligent, as much as possible	**N1** 粘 sticky, glutinous, greasy, persevere

怠 (N5) neglect, laziness	**賀** (N1) congratulations, joy	**庄** (N1) level	**鴻** (N1) large bird, wild goose
強 (N1) strong	**軍** (N1) army, force, troops, war, battle	**惨** (N1) wretched, disaster, cruelty, harsh	**篤** (N1) fervent, kind, cordial, serious, deliberate
静 (N1) quiet	**造** (N1) create, make, structure, physique	**陶** (N1) pottery, porcelain	**植** (N1) plant
又 (N1) or again, furthermore, on the other hand	**倉** (N1) godown, warehouse, storehouse, cellar, treasury	**奉** (N1) observance, offer, present, dedicate	**圧** (N1) pressure, push, overwhelm, oppress, dominate
唇 (N1) lips	**経** (N1) sutra, longitude, pass thru, expire, warp	**楊** (N1) willow	**販** (N1) marketing, sell, trade

遠 (N5) distant, far	**社** (N1) company, firm, office, association, shrine	**牲** (N1) animal sacrifice, offering	**聴** (N1) listen, headstrong, naughty, careful inquiry
偶 (N1) accidentally, even number, couple, man & wife	**守** (N1) guard, protect, defend, obey	**嫁** (N1) marry into, bride	**占** (N1) fortune-telling, divining, forecasting, occupy
磁 (N1) magnet, porcelain	**滉** (N1) deep and broad	**衰** (N1) decline, wane, weaken	**枚** (N1) sheet of..., counter for flat thin objects or sheets
収 (N1) income, obtain, reap, pay, supply, store	**漸** (N1) steadily, gradually advancing, finally, barely	**涙** (N1) tears, sympathy	**跳** (N1) hop, leap up, spring, jerk, prance, buck, splash
群 (N1) flock, group, crowd, herd, swarm, cluster	**築** (N1) fabricate, build, construct	**嫌** (N1) dislike, detest, hate	**払** (N1) pay, clear out, prune, banish, dispose of

洗 (N5)	**仁** (N1)	**御** (N1)	**革** (N1)
wash, inquire into, probe	humanity, virtue, benevolence, charity, man, kernel	honorable, manipulate, govern	leather, become serious, skin, hide, pelt
伸 (N1)	**草** (N1)	**隼** (N1)	**急** (N1)
expand, stretch, extend, lengthen, increase	grass, weeds, herbs, pasture, write, draft	falcon	hurry, emergency, sudden, steep
効 (N1)	**心** (N1)	**監** (N1)	**剰** (N1)
merit, efficacy, efficiency, benefit	heart, mind, spirit	oversee, official, govt office, rule, administer	surplus, besides
練 (N1)	**嘆** (N1)	**応** (N1)	**竜** (N1)
practice, gloss, train, drill, polish, refine	sigh, lament, moan, grieve	apply, answer, yes, OK, reply, accept	dragon, imperial
敷 (N1)	**藻** (N1)	**亡** (N1)	**頼** (N1)
spread, pave, sit, promulgate	seaweed, duckweed	deceased, the late, dying, perish	trust, request

梅 N5	米 N1	簡 N1	崇 N1
plum	rice, USA, metre	simplicity, brevity	adore, respect, revere, worship
念 N1	随 N1	叡 N1	館 N1
wish, sense, idea, thought, feeling, desire	follow, though, notwithstanding	intelligence, imperial	building, mansion, large building, palace
肢 N1	門 N1	遇 N1	屈 N1
limb, arms & legs	gates	interview, treat, entertain, receive, deal with	yield, bend, flinch, submit
族 N1	絃 N1	搾 N1	黙 N1
tribe, family	string, cord, samisen music	squeeze	silence, become silent, stop speaking, leave as is
追 N1	衡 N1	渉 N1	升 N1
chase, drive away, follow, pursue, meanwhile	equilibrium, measuring rod, scale	ford, ferry, port	measuring box, 1.8 liter

N3	N1	N1	N1
阻	同	柊	末
thwart, separate from, prevent, obstruct, deter	same, agree, equal	holly	end, close, tip, powder, posterity

N1	N1	N1	N1
喝	八	触	困
hoarse, scold	eight	contact, touch, feel, hit, proclaim, announce	quandary, become distressed, annoyed

N1	N1	N1	N1
辞	調	霜	拐
resign, word, term, expression	tune, tone, meter, key (music), writing style	frost	kidnap, falsify

N1	N1	N1	N1
池	乱	置	乾
pond, cistern, pool, reservoir	riot, war, disorder, disturb	placement, put, set, deposit, leave behind	drought, dry, dessicate, drink up, heaven, emperor

N1	N1	N1	N1
俸	需	陳	味
stipend, salary	demand, request, need	exhibit, state, relate, explain	flavor, taste

閉 N5 closed, shut	**繊** N1 slender, fine, thin kimono	**果** N1 fruit, reward, carry out, achieve, complete, end	**科** N1 department, course, section
奔 N1 bustle, run	**洵** N1 alike, truth	**物** N1 thing, object, matter	**症** N1 symptoms, illness
鳩 N1 pigeon, dove	**吏** N1 officer, an official	**頑** N1 stubborn, foolish, firmly	**隠** N1 conceal, hide, cover
悟 N1 enlightenment, perceive, discern, realize	**蓮** N1 lotus	**香** N1 incense, smell, perfume	**蒸** N1 steam, heat, sultry, foment, get musty
虐 N1 tyrannize, oppress	**会** N1 meeting, meet, party, association, interview, join	**疾** N1 rapidly	**馨** N1 fragrant, balmy, favourable

詩 (N3)	裸 (N1)	彼 (N1)	並 (N1)
poem, poetry	naked, nude, uncovered, partially clothed	he, that, the	row, and, besides, as well as, line up, rank with
端 (N1)	浩 (N1)	魚 (N1)	大 (N1)
edge, origin, end, point, border, verge, cape	wide expanse, abundance, vigorous	fish	large, big
劾 (N1)	鉄 (N1)	鋭 (N1)	戸 (N1)
censure, criminal investigation	iron	pointed, sharpness, edge, weapon, sharp, violent	door
閣 (N1)	窯 (N1)	来 (N1)	譜 (N1)
tower, tall building, palace	kiln, oven, furnace	come, due, next, cause, become	musical score, music, note, staff, table, genealogy
梢 (N1)	後 (N1)	継 (N1)	譲 (N1)
treetops, twig	behind, back, later	inherit, succeed, patch, graft (tree)	defer, turnover, transfer, convey

雑 N5	寄 N1	資 N1	頒 N1
miscellaneous	draw near, stop in, bring near, gather, collect	assets, resources, capital, funds, data	distribute, disseminate, partition, understand
乏 N1	毅 N1	耀 N1	転 N1
destitution, scarce, limited	strong	shine, sparkle, gleam, twinkle	revolve, turn around, change
蛮 N1	星 N1	申 N1	把 N1
barbarian	star, spot, dot, mark	have the honor to, sign of the monkey, 3-5PM	grasp, faggot, bunch, counter for bundles
糸 N1	段 N1	線 N1	上 N1
thread	grade, steps, stairs	line, track	above, up
血 N1	伎 N1	禅 N1	勧 N1
blood	deed, skill	Zen, silent meditation	persuade, recommend, advise, encourage, offer

郡 (N5) county, district	**璃** (N1) glassy, lapis lazuli	**矛** (N1) halberd, arms, festival float	**寅** (N1) sign of the tiger, 3-5AM
符 (N1) token, sign, mark, tally, charm	**逸** (N1) deviate, idleness, leisure, miss the mark, evade	**索** (N1) cord, rope	**刻** (N1) engrave, cut fine, chop, hash, mince, time, carving
繕 (N1) darning, repair, mend, trim, tidy up, adjust	**原** (N1) meadow, original, primitive, field, plain	**襟** (N1) collar, neck, lapel	**短** (N1) short, brevity, fault, defect, weak point
施 (N1) alms, apply bandages, administer first-aid	**試** (N1) test, try, attempt, experiment, ordeal	**衣** (N1) garment, clothes, dressing	**私** (N1) private, I, me
犬 (N1) dog	**典** (N1) code, ceremony, law, rule	**曙** (N1) dawn, daybreak	**歌** (N1) song, sing

洋 (N5) ocean, western style	**頌** (N1) eulogy	**傍** (N1) bystander, side, besides, while, nearby, 3rd person	**陵** (N1) mausoleum, imperial tomb
税 (N1) tax, duty	**幣** (N1) cash, bad habit, humble prefix, gift	**複** (N1) duplicate, double, compound, multiple	**束** (N1) bundle, sheaf, ream, tie in bundles, govern
擊 (N1) beat, attack, defeat, conquer	**裝** (N1) attire, dress, pretend, disguise, profess	**遙** (N1) far off, distant, long ago	**覽** (N1) perusal, see
師 (N1) expert, teacher, master, army, war	**網** (N1) netting, network	**達** (N1) accomplished, reach, arrive, attain	**墾** (N1) ground-breaking, open up farmland
柚 (N1) citron	**鳳** (N1) male mythical bird	**妊** (N1) pregnancy	**属** (N1) belong, genus, subordinate official, affiliated

N5	N1	N1	N1
盆 basin, lantern festival, tray	啄 peck, pick up	勇 courage, cheer up, be in high spirits, bravery	習 learn
N1	**N1**	**N1**	**N1**
萌 show symptoms of, sprout, bud, malt	快 cheerful, pleasant, agreeable, comfortable	癖 mannerism, habit, vice, trait, fault, kink	躍 leap, dance, skip
N1	**N1**	**N1**	**N1**
赴 proceed, get, become, tend	性 sex, gender, nature	介 jammed in, shellfish, mediate, concern oneself with	軽 lightly, trifling, unimportant
N1	**N1**	**N1**	**N1**
喜 rejoice, take pleasure in	為 do, change, make, benefit	偉 admirable, greatness, remarkable, conceited	磨 grind, polish, scour, improve, brush (teeth)
N1	**N1**	**N1**	**N1**
職 post, employment, work	虫 insect, bug, temper	鉛 lead	近 near, early, akin, tantamount

光 N5 ray, light	**鮎** N1 freshwater trout, smelt	**鼓** N1 drum, beat, rouse, muster	**康** N1 ease, peace
災 N1 disaster, calamity, woe, curse, evil	**妻** N1 wife, spouse	**労** N1 labor, thank for, reward for, toil, trouble	**紗** N1 gauze, gossamer
仙 N1 hermit, wizard, cent	**封** N1 seal, closing	**容** N1 contain, form, looks	**絵** N1 picture, drawing, painting, sketch
刺 N1 thorn, pierce, stab, prick, sting, calling card	**樺** N1 birch	**糾** N1 twist, ask, investigate, verify	**皇** N1 emperor
知 N1 know, wisdom	**披** N1 expose, open	**那** N1 what?	**負** N1 defeat, negative, -, minus, bear, owe

矢	幼	峰	坪
N1	N1	N1	N1
dart, arrow	infancy, childhood	summit, peak	two-mat area, ~36 sq ft

浴	術	食	苑
N1	N1	N1	N1
bathe, be favored with, bask in	art, technique, skill, means, trick, resources	eat, food	garden, farm, park

淡	祖	熊	尼
N1	N1	N1	N1
thin, faint, pale, fleeting	ancestor, pioneer, founder	bear	nun

綱	絶	伯	住
N1	N1	N1	N1
hawser, class (genus), rope, cord, cable	discontinue, beyond, sever, cut off, abstain	chief, count, earl, uncle, Brazil	dwell, reside, live, inhabit

艦	碧	弥	保
N1	N1	N1	N1
warship	blue, green	all the more, increasingly	protect, guarantee, keep, preserve, sustain, support

Kanji	Level	Meaning
沢	N5	swamp
嬢	N1	lass, girl, Miss, daughter
汁	N1	soup, juice, broth, sap, gravy, pus
聖	N1	holy, saint, sage, master, priest
摩	N1	chafe, rub, polish, grind, scrape
眠	N1	sleep, die, sleepy
碑	N1	tombstone, monument
炭	N1	charcoal, coal
翌	N1	the following, next
獲	N1	seize, get, find, earn, acquire, can, may, able to
振	N1	shake, wave, wag, swing
礼	N1	salute, bow, ceremony, thanks, remuneration
晨	N1	morning, early
攻	N1	aggression, attack
席	N1	seat, mat, occasion, place
微	N1	delicate, minuteness, insignificance
削	N1	plane, sharpen, whittle, pare
奨	N1	exhort, urge, encourage
支	N1	branch, support, sustain
雷	N1	thunder, lightening bolt

雛 (N5) chick, squab, duckling, doll	**布** (N1) linen, cloth	**臓** (N1) entrails, viscera, bowels	**柔** (N1) tender, weakness, gentleness, softness
流 (N1) current, a sink, flow, forfeit	**開** (N1) open, unfold, unseal	**徹** (N1) penetrate, clear, pierce, strike home	**部** (N1) section, bureau, dept, class, copy, part
殿 (N1) Mr., hall, mansion, palace, temple, lord	**南** (N1) south	**鎌** (N1) sickle, scythe, trick	**莉** (N1) jasmine
諾 (N1) consent, assent, agreement	**殴** (N1) assault, hit, beat, thrash	**酸** (N1) acid, bitterness, sour, tart	**憾** (N1) remorse, regret, be sorry
類 (N1) sort, kind, variety, class, genus	**息** (N1) breath, respiration, son, interest (on money)	**促** (N1) stimulate, urge, press, demand, incite	**袋** (N1) sack, bag, pouch

凱	襲	半	奥
victory song	attack, advance on, succeed to, pile, heap	half, middle, odd number, semi-, part-half	heart, interior
史	仰	店	勤
history, chronicle	face-up, look up, depend, seek, respect, rever	store, shop	diligence, become employed, serve
眼	渡	槙	拒
eyeball	transit, ford, ferry, cross, import, deliver	twig, ornamental evergreen	repel, refuse, reject, decline
骨	栄	堪	侮
skeleton, bone, remains, frame	flourish, prosperity, honor, glory, splendor	withstand, endure, support, resist	scorn, despise, make light of, contempt
中	許	財	穏
in, inside, middle, mean, center	permit, approve	property, money, wealth, assets	calm, quiet, moderation

畝 (N5) furrow, 30 tsubo, ridge, rib	**操** (N1) maneuver, manipulate, operate, steer, chastity	**轄** (N1) control, wedge	**消** (N1) extinguish, blow out, turn off, neutralize, cancel
挑 (N1) challenge, contend for, make love to	**了** (N1) complete, finish	**悪** (N1) bad, vice, rascal, false, evil, wrong	**荷** (N1) baggage, shoulder-pole load
貸 (N1) lend	**堅** (N1) strict, hard, solid, tough, tight, reliable	**補** (N1) supplement, supply, make good, offset, compensate	**婿** (N1) bridegroom, son-in-law
崎 (N1) promontory, cape, spit	**騰** (N1) inflation, advancing, going	**養** (N1) foster, bring up, rear, develop, nurture	**仏** (N1) Buddha, the dead, France
待 (N1) wait, depend on	**北** (N1) north	**借** (N1) borrow, rent	**拾** (N1) pick up, gather, find, go on foot, ten

N5

day, sun, Japan

N5

day, sun, Japan

N5

day, sun, Japan

N5

day, sun, Japan

N5

day, sun, Japan

N5

day, sun, Japan

N5

day, sun, Japan

N5

day, sun, Japan

N5

day, sun, Japan

N5

day, sun, Japan

N5

day, sun, Japan

N5

day, sun, Japan

N5

day, sun, Japan

N5

day, sun, Japan

N5

day, sun, Japan

N5

day, sun, Japan

N5

day, sun, Japan

N5

day, sun, Japan

N5

day, sun, Japan

N5

day, sun, Japan

N5	N5	N5	N5
日 day, sun, Japan	日 day, sun, Japan	日 day, sun, Japan	日 day, sun, Japan
日 day, sun, Japan	日 day, sun, Japan	日 day, sun, Japan	日 day, sun, Japan
日 day, sun, Japan	日 day, sun, Japan	日 day, sun, Japan	日 day, sun, Japan
日 day, sun, Japan	日 day, sun, Japan	日 day, sun, Japan	日 day, sun, Japan